All About Your
BLADDER

Marne Ventura and Maria Koran

www.av2books.com

AV² provides enriched content that supplements and complements this book. Weigl's AV² books strive to create inspired learning and engage young minds in a total learning experience.

Your AV² Media Enhanced books come alive with...

Audio
Listen to sections of the book read aloud.

Key Words
Study vocabulary, and complete a matching word activity.

Video
Watch informative video clips.

Quizzes
Test your knowledge.

Embedded Weblinks
Gain additional information for research.

Slide Show
View images and captions, and prepare a presentation.

Try This!
Complete activities and hands-on experiments.

... and much, much more!

Go to **www.av2books.com**, and enter this book's unique code.

BOOK CODE

W649336

AV² by Weigl brings you media enhanced books that support active learning.

Published by AV² by Weigl
350 5th Avenue, 59th Floor
New York, NY 10118
Website: www.av2books.com

Library of Congress Cataloging-in-Publication Data

Names: Ventura, Marne, author. | Koran, Maria, author.
Title: Bladder / Marne Ventura and Maria Koran.
Description: New York, NY : AV2 by Weigl, [2017] | Series: All about your...
 | Includes bibliographical references and index.
Identifiers: LCCN 2016034623 (print) | LCCN 2016035179 (ebook) | ISBN
 9781489651259 (hard cover : alk. paper) | ISBN 9781489651266 (soft cover :
 alk. paper) | ISBN 9781489651273 (Multi-user ebk.)
Subjects: LCSH: Bladder--Juvenile literature. | Bladder--Diseases--Juvenile
 literature.
Classification: LCC RC919 .V46 2017 (print) | LCC RC919 (ebook) | DDC
 616.6/2--dc23
LC record available at https://lccn.loc.gov/2016034623

Printed in the United States of America in Brainerd, Minnesota
1 2 3 4 5 6 7 8 9 0 20 19 18 17 16

082016
210716

Project Coordinator: Piper Whelan   Art Director: Terry Paulhus

Every reasonable effort has been made to trace ownership and to obtain permission to reprint copyright material. The publishers would be pleased to have any errors or omissions brought to their attention so that they may be corrected in subsequent printings.

Weigl acknowledges Getty Images and Alamy as its primary image suppliers for this title.

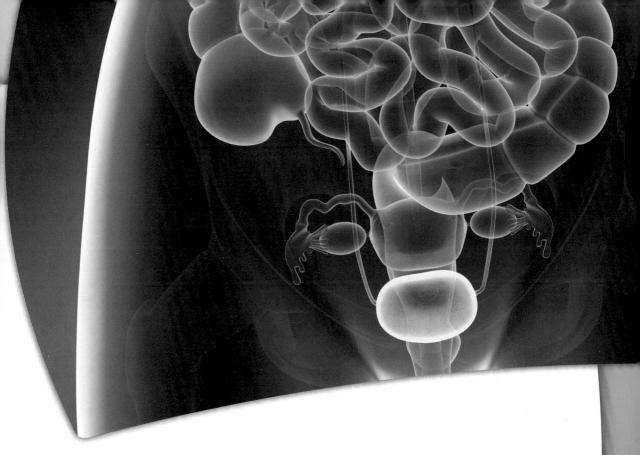

Contents

Chapter 1

What Is a Bladder?

The **organs** inside your body are always hard at work. Each organ belongs to a **system** with a special job. Your bladder is an organ in the urinary system. This system filters waste from the blood, which makes **urine**. Your bladder holds the urine until it leaves your body.

Put your hands on your hips. Do you feel the top of your **pelvic bone**? It is shaped like a bowl. Your bladder rests at the bottom of the bowl.

The bladder is made of smooth muscle. Smooth muscles are arranged in layers. The bladder is also an **involuntary** muscle. These are muscles that work without your control. Involuntary muscles do their work on their own. Your stomach muscles are also involuntary muscles.

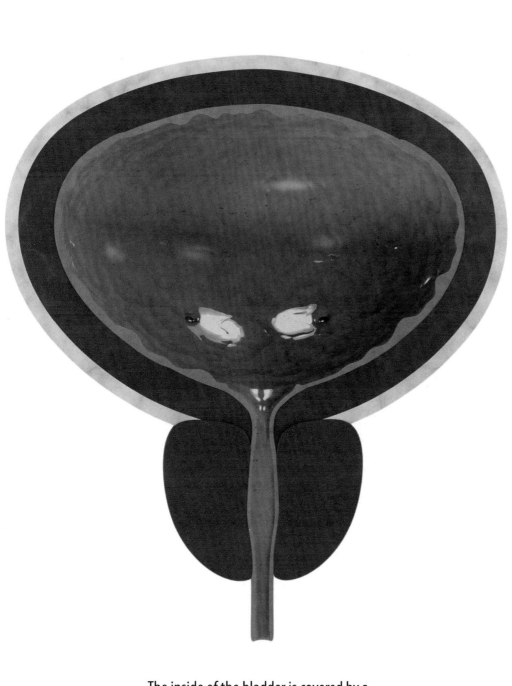

The inside of the bladder is covered by a smooth surface. It is called the mucosa.

Water balloons expand as they fill with fluid.

Your bladder works like a water balloon. As your bladder fills with urine, it stretches to a bigger size. Your bladder goes back to a smaller size after you urinate.

A healthy bladder can hold 16 ounces (473 milliliters) of urine. That is like a very large glass of water. The bladder is about the size and shape of a pear.

An eight year old will make about 1 quart (1 liter) of urine every day.

Chapter 2

What Does a Bladder Do?

The urinary system has many parts including the bladder. The system has two **kidneys**, two **ureters**, and one **urethra**. The kidneys are very important. Kidneys filter waste from your blood. These bean-shaped organs are the size of your fist. One kidney sits on each side of your body.

Blood is sent to the kidneys by the heart. The heart is always pumping blood through your body. More than 1 quart (1 L) of blood is sent to your kidneys every minute.

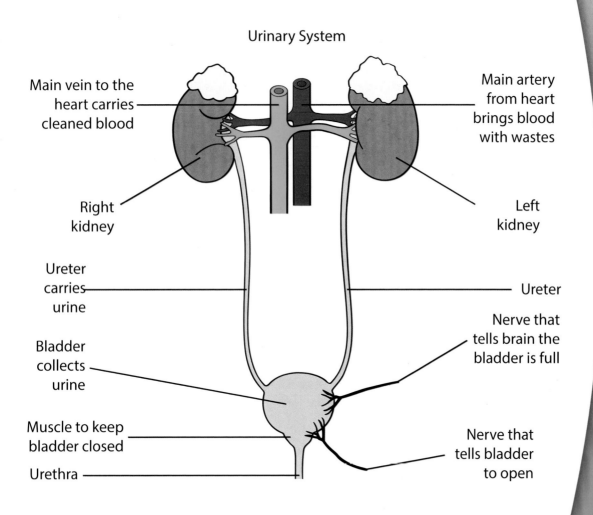

Urinary System

Main vein to the heart carries cleaned blood

Main artery from heart brings blood with wastes

Right kidney

Left kidney

Ureter carries urine

Ureter

Nerve that tells brain the bladder is full

Bladder collects urine

Muscle to keep bladder closed

Nerve that tells bladder to open

Urethra

Tiny bundles of blood vessels work inside the kidneys. These vessels clean the blood as it passes through the kidneys. The vessels separate waste, extra water, and salt from the blood, which all become urine.

Urine is made up of four types of waste. One type of waste is made as your body breaks down food. The second type is made as the body breaks down muscle. The third type of waste is **ammonia**, which is a gas your body makes as it breaks down **protein**. The fourth type is a fluid made by the liver called **bile**. Urine also includes water, salt, and a product that makes it yellow called **urochrome**.

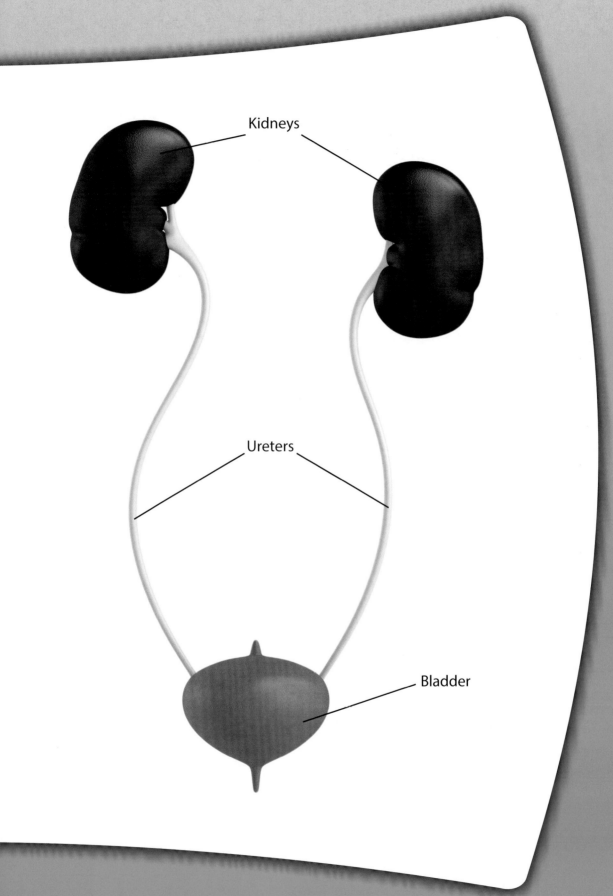

Kidneys

Ureters

Bladder

Urine leaves the kidneys through one of the ureters. This long tube leads to the bladder. Urine flows down the ureter and into the bladder. The bladder holds the urine until it leaves the body.

The urethra leads out of the base of the bladder. Two muscles circle the urethra. These muscles work like a rubber band. The muscles keep the urine inside your bladder until you urinate.

Nerves send a signal to your brain when your bladder is full. You feel the need to empty your bladder. Your brain tells the urethra muscles to relax. It tells the bladder muscles to tighten. You squeeze the urine out of your bladder. The urine goes through the urethra and into the toilet.

Urine has no odor when it is inside the bladder. Bacteria in the air cause urine to smell.

It is important to go to the bathroom when you feel the urge. Holding in urine for too long can make you sick.

Chapter 3
Why Do I Need a Bladder?

The bladder is the storage tank for urine. It lets you hold and get rid of urine. As your body turns food into energy, it makes waste. As your body grows and repairs itself, it makes waste. Your kidneys turn waste, extra water, and salt into urine. If waste stayed in your blood, it could make you sick.

The urinary system could not do its job without the bladder. The bladder helps keep your body clean and helps you get rid of waste.

Keeping the kidneys and the bladder healthy will also keep the rest of the body healthy and strong.

A ureter is about 10-12 inches long (25-30 centimeters) and about 1/8 inch (3-4 mm) in diameter.

Chapter 4
Problems with the Bladder

Most bladders work as they should. Sometimes there are problems with the bladder.

A baby's bladder fills and empties on its own. The baby has not learned to control its bladder. Most children's brains learn to control their bladder by four years old.

It takes longer for some children to learn control. They might wet the bed at night, or the child might have an accident during the day. Many things can cause loss of bladder control. Children who wet their beds may have a small bladder. Their bladder gets too full if they sleep for a long time. The nerves going to the brain might still be developing. The bladder muscles might also still be developing. Children usually outgrow bladder control problems. Doctors can provide exercises or lifestyle changes that help.

Not drinking a big glass of water before bed may help prevent bed wetting.

Another bladder problem can be caused by an infection. This can happen when germs get inside your body and make you sick.

You might feel the need to urinate more when you have a bladder infection. It might burn or itch when you urinate. Doctors prescribe antibiotics to cure the infection.

Sometimes a kidney cannot do its job. Sometimes both kidneys do not work right. Every person needs one working kidney. If both kidneys do not work, surgeons can do a kidney transplant. In this operation, a healthy kidney is removed from one person and given to a person whose kidneys are not working. Both people can be healthy if they each have one good kidney.

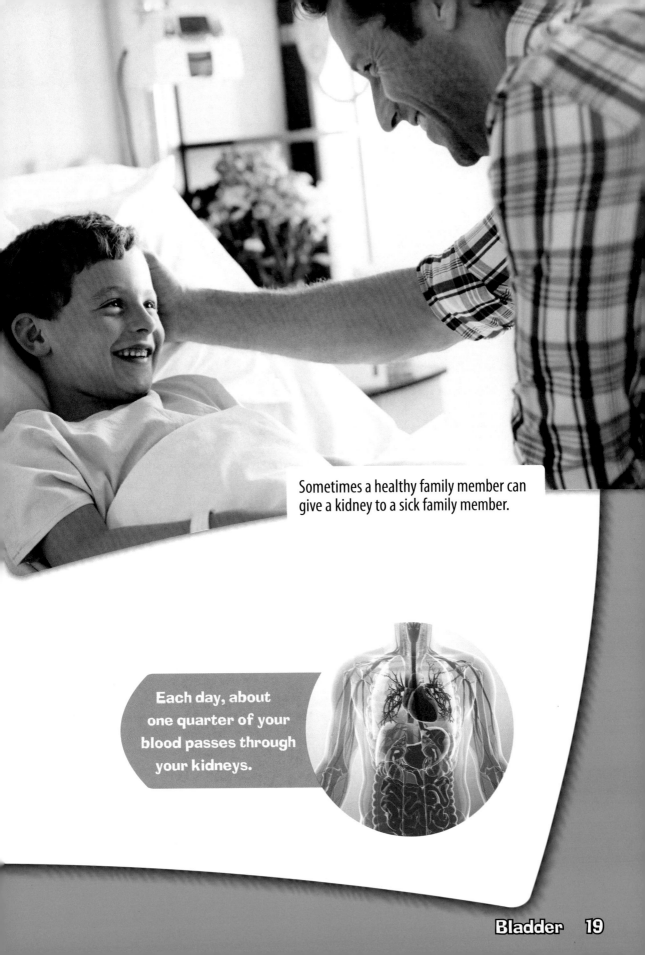

Sometimes a healthy family member can give a kidney to a sick family member.

Each day, about one quarter of your blood passes through your kidneys.

Chapter 5
Keeping the Bladder Healthy

Taking care of your bladder is easy. There are a few simple rules to follow.

It is important to drink enough fluids. Water is the best choice. Water helps all parts of your body do a better job. It also helps prevent bladder infections. It is important to drink extra water if it is hot outside. If you are exercising, you should drink more water, too.

Newborn babies are about 78 percent water. By one year old, they are 65 percent water.

Strawberries are made up of 92 percent water.

It is also important to take a shower every day. Try to avoid using bubble bath soap. This soap can cause a bladder infection. Wearing clean clothes is also a good idea. Being clean will get rid of bacteria that might cause a bladder infection. Urinate right away when you need to, and empty your bladder completely. This will also help to prevent bladder infections.

Eating fresh fruits and vegetables is also good for your bladder. These foods have a lot of water in them. Fruits and vegetables also have vitamins and fiber that keep you healthy.

Quiz

1. **What kind of muscles work on their own, without your control?**

2. **What system is the bladder a part of?**

3. **What do the kidneys do?**

4. **How many types of waste make up urine?**

5. **How many working kidneys does a person need to be healthy?**

6. **How much of your blood passes through your kidneys each day?**

7. **When do most children's brains learn to control their bladder?**

8. **What materials do the kidneys turn into urine?**

9. **How much blood is sent to your kidneys every minute?**

10. **Where is the bladder found in the body?**

10. AT THE BOTTOM OF THE PELVIC BONE
9. MORE THAN 1 QUART
8. WASTE, EXTRA WATER, AND SALT
7. BY FOUR YEARS OLD
6. ABOUT ONE QUARTER OF YOUR BLOOD

5. ONE
4. FOUR
3. THEY FILTER WASTE FROM THE BLOOD
2. THE URINARY SYSTEM
1. INVOLUNTARY MUSCLES

ANSWERS

Key Words

ammonia: a gas made when the body breaks down protein

bile: a liquid made by the liver

involuntary: done automatically or without control

kidneys: two bean-shaped organs that filter waste from the blood and produce urine

organs: groups of tissues that perform a special job

pelvic bone: a part of the skeleton that is made up of three hip bones

protein: a substance found in all living things

system: a group of organs or parts that work together

ureters: the tubes through which urine flows from the kidney to the bladder

urethra: the tube through which urine leaves the bladder

urine: fluid waste created by the kidneys as they filter blood

urochrome: a breakdown product of the blood

Index

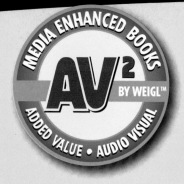

Log on to www.av2books.com

AV² by Weigl brings you media enhanced books that support active learning. Go to www.av2books.com, and enter the special code found on page 2 of this book. You will gain access to enriched and enhanced content that supplements and complements this book. Content includes video, audio, weblinks, quizzes, a slide show, and activities.

AV² Online Navigation

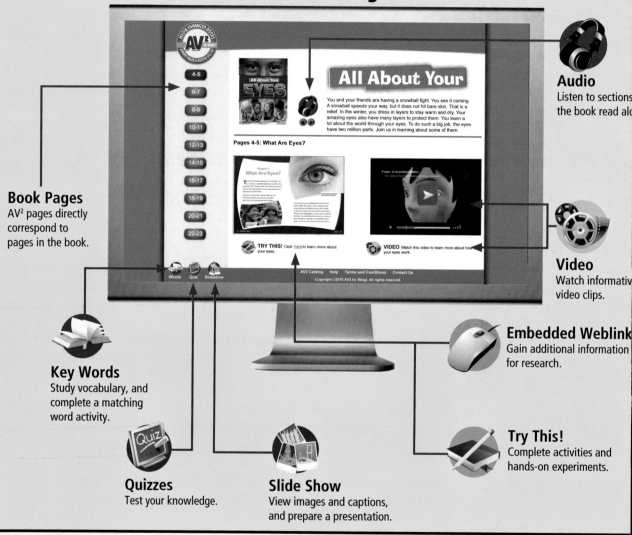

Book Pages
AV² pages directly correspond to pages in the book.

Audio
Listen to sections the book read alo

Video
Watch informativ video clips.

Embedded Weblink
Gain additional information for research.

Key Words
Study vocabulary, and complete a matching word activity.

Try This!
Complete activities and hands-on experiments.

Quizzes
Test your knowledge.

Slide Show
View images and captions, and prepare a presentation.

AV² was built to bridge the gap between print and digital. We encourage you to tell us what you like and what you want to see in the future.

Sign up to be an AV² Ambassador at www.av2books.com/ambassador.

Due to the dynamic nature of the Internet, some of the URLs and activities provided as part of AV² by Weigl may have changed or ceased to exist. AV² by Weigl accepts no responsibility for any such changes. All media enhanced books are regularly monitored to update addresses and sites in a timely manner. Contact AV² by Weigl at 1-866-649-3445 or av2books@weigl.com with any questions, comments, or feedback.